CRANK IT UP!

Crank It Up!

MLB Batting Illustrated

Willie Mays

By

J.A. PATRINA

About The Author

Joe Patrina is a singer/songwriter based in West Simsbury, Connecticut, where he leads the popular country/rock group LittleHouse. As with his songwriting, Joe applies his seasoned observational skills and to-the-point writing style to pen insightful works on sports, history, politics, law, medicine, and music.

A co-founder of Wall Street Systems, Joe brings his lifetime of experience at a global level to his musical and literary endeavors.

ISBN: 978-1-7330672-7-0   [Paperback Edition]

Please visit *hoodwinked.net* for video versions of this manuscript.
Printed and bound in The United States of America.

Published by LittleHouse Enterprises Inc.

Frank Thomas, White Sox, 7 straight years batting over .300, with 20-plus homers, 100 RBIs and 100 walks (foot floats with follow through). Inducted in 2014.

Sadaharu Oh
Cranked and loaded!

A Ty Cobb Bat (note 40-T.C.)

Contents

The Miracle League

A few years ago, Scott Franklin, a friend of mine, raised money to build a small, rubber-matted baseball field in West Hartford, Connecticut - designed accessible to special needs children. This way any kid, even one in a wheel chair, could experience the American pastime and have their moment in the sun.

The Connecticut field is just one of many across America, operated by one of the country's great charities – *The Miracle League*.

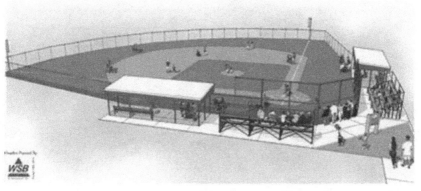

March, 2016 - A Miracle League Field

I was honored to write and sing an opening-day song during the ribbon cutting ceremony at the West Hartford field. Sounding a bit like Johnny Cash, I sang, surrounded by all of the darling children who would soon make it their home.

The song "We Play Baseball in America", found at the end of the book, was refined with the help of Scott Franklin.

As you will soon read - by chance - I subsequently met Hall of Famer, Rickey Henderson, who clued me in to the "hidden art of batting baseballs". I wrote this book as a result of the Henderson encounter. In doing so I initially thought of the very fit, athletic, 15-year old boys I instruct, but I never forgot those other kids.

And so, this book, written for any American wanting a peek inside the amazing world of MLB batting, is dedicated to *The Miracle League,* with book sale proceeds going to the charity.

J.A. Patrina

Ricky Henderson

As said, I tie this book to Rickey Henderson, a hall of famer, with whom I had the aforementioned impromptu discussion.

In 2014 an Off Broadway play ran called *The Bronx Bombers* about the legendary 1978 incident where Reggie Jackson and Billy Martin "made contact" in the Yankee dugout.

Yogi (Berra) and Thurman (Munson) needed to "fix things" before the boss George (Steinbrenner) stepped in.

I was thrilled that my friend Glen Feigen, having access to tickets, arranged for me <u>and</u> my fourteen-year-old "Yankee-son" Joseph to attend this first showing of *The Bronx Bombers*.

Luckily for me and everyone else there, Brandon Steiner of *Steiner Sports Memorabilia* hosted opening night. Brandon and a bunch of Yankee greats, including: Bobby Richardson, Bucky Dent, Joe Pepitone, Tino Martinez and Rickey Henderson, highlighted the pre-show cocktail bash.

After a few lively discussions with Brandon and the first four Yankee heroes, I eventually settled into a "technical" chat with Rickey – about batting.

At the time I was working with a few teenage boys, trying to convert them from hand-and-arm, little league swingers into classic MLB rotational hitters. Right there in the theater lobby I showed Rickey my hitting instruction program and explained the principles behind the form I advocate.

Rickey said I set up and rotated correctly, but based upon my explanation, he surmised that I did not truly understand the principle behind my correct swing. I knew the rules, but not the reason.

Yes, you set up well, and your hands and elbows move together near the body as you make the turn, he noted, *but the reason you are squaring up correctly is that your stance makes you pivot through your core on your front shoulder, and the shoulder pivot then squares you up to the incoming ball.*

Huh? Then I stepped through what he described.

In all my years of swinging a bat, this key insight – how the stance and step cause the squaring up, power result – never occurred to me. Plus, I never realized I pivoted on the front shoulder and turned with my core, not my arms.

I had grown up merely copying the exact styles of my favorite hitters, which is probably why my swing mechanics are good, but I had never analyzed it very deeply.

Instead, as a kid, I assumed each MLB star's style different, but now Rickey made me realize that most of the great MLB hitters share a fundamental principle in kind. If one's stance is formed properly, then when stepping to strike the ball, one will use the stomach (core) to pivot on the front shoulder, allowing the back hip to swing around the front hip, like a gate on a fence post. Gates turn; they don't spin.

Suddenly I saw it. All of my young students were "spinners" rather than "batters". Instead of the front shoulder, their relaxed upper body stances caused the pivot post to run from their head down through the center of the body, between the legs and to the ground. This center axis stayed fixed, and the hands and arms just made a big circle around the centerline like a ballet dancer. Rather than pivot, they pirouetted – their core barely engaged.

And more, to stay stable during the pirouette, the young hitters barely took a step, if at all. As a result, they did not "bat" with their whole body; they "hit" with their hands, squashing bugs with their twisted feet and letting the bat fly away at the end of the spin, just to keep them from falling over.

The Crank, Step and Go Stages

After this, Rickey and I covered other ground in more detail, such as the **'stance'** stage, which locks the upper body in place so that it can only pivot around the front shoulder, the **"step"** stage, where one's load on the back leg and stride on the front leg builds the power supply needed to drive the ball, keeping the hands back as the core makes the first move, and the **"go"** stage where pent up energy is released in a squaring up manner, perpendicular to the incoming ball – the whole body involved.

Funny thing, Rickey and I never discussed base stealing, though Rickey is the top guy of all times. Instead, he started to describe his conditioning regimen to my son, feeling we ought to value this first, considering his avoidance of injury across 28 years of professional baseball. Rickey is pure knowhow, and now he had passed a little know-how on to me. *Thanks!*

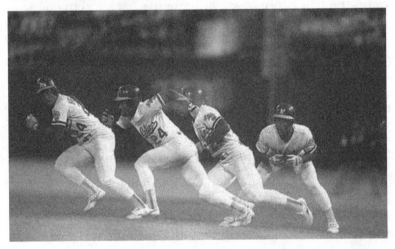

Moments later, upon telling my host and friend Glen Feigen about the conversation I just had with Rickey, Glen explained the stance position described by Rickey as a three dimensional "crank" twist of the upper body, and I decided to use the word "crank", instead of "stance" or "coil" as it more accurately described what was happening.

Crank, step and go ... the professionals really know how to boil it all down (above, before the show: Henderson, Pepitone, Dent, Richardson and Martinez).

Then the bell rang and we were all asked to enter the theater for the show. BTW, the show was magnificent.

PART 1
CRANK, STEP & GO DEFINED

Trying It Out

Back home, with the simplified *Crank, Step* and *Go* stages in mind, I re-watched the You-tube films of the great hitters of yesterday and today, and realized how each facet of a contiguous professional swing – the *crank's* upper body form and back leg load, the *step's* toe angle and back-to-front weight transfer through the stomach, and the *go's* ball striking and follow through dynamics – are but micro-by-products of the three main body forms: *Crank, Step and Go.*

If one gets the *Crank, Step and Go* body forms right, then all of the micro-details fall into place. No wonder they can hit a ball coming in at 95 mph!

Since my encounter with Rickey, I subsequently found myself working with 15/16-year old boys committed to the game. I attempted to get some of the boys to break their old little league habits: arm-led, spinning swings where they lean backwards on their back foot while "hitting".

I tried the streamlined, 3-step approach out on a few teens. Some got it pretty quickly, though in many cases it took repeated sessions in the cage using tee and soft toss exercises to break old habits. But others simply could not grasp it after merely hearing my description and staring at a few You Tube films.

So I decided to write the *crank, step and go* formula down, and rather than illustrate it with fast moving film, I would use still shots of the great hitters to frame the principles. These still shots constitute the book's format.

In the end, as you will see, this is not "my" way of batting; it's how <u>most</u> of the greats bat. I just simplified the batting dots down to the three actual stages and connected them.

Indeed, after going through the coming pages, you will likely conclude that all of these great stars basically look the same. But that is exactly the point. They collectively embody the book's illustrations and so should you - if you want to optimize your natural athleticism.

Alternatively, to believe that, next to this illustrious crew of MLB greats, you ought to develop your own personal methodology ... becomes sheer folly. Your unorthodox method will certainly work, but it might deliver a 260 batting average instead of the 310 average you have within.

And yes there are the exceptions like Yogi Berra, Lou Pinella and Mark McGwire who did quite well with idiosyncratic methods, but this does not lead to the universal conclusion that batting is strictly personal, with thousands of valid styles to choose from.

McGwire's spin form

You will also find that while the *crank, step and go* forms are consistent across most batters, that it is the player's body shape, their pitch-by-pitch decisions, their intensity of the turn, governed by the size of the step (swing tempo factors), that makes a Wade Boggs look different from a Reggie Jackson.

One more point, at first, this book solely explored form, not the realm of situational hitting – the chess game between hitters and their pitcher/catcher opponents. But while writing the book's draft, sitting in the lobby of the Lowes Hotel in Miami ... someone came up behind me and said, "That's Willie Mays."

The commentator, Phil Rosen, told me he played hardball until age 40 and that he had been the owner of a baseball team (The Navigators, in Lynn, Massachusetts). We started talking, me about form, and he about situational hitting. We would have talked for hours but his wife said he had to go.

Then it dawned on me, upon finishing the batting part of the book, I might add a word or two about "Situational Hitting".

And it came to be.

PART 2
MECHANICS ILLUSTRATED

A D1 college player all "cranked up" and ready to go.
Front shoulder pulled down and forward, rear shoulder pulled up, and back.

The Crank Stage

The Crank is the position one assumes when in the stance. Most young players have never experienced the crank because it is intellectually <u>multi-dimensional</u> and physically uncomfortable, plus no one they know ever described it.

Dimension 1 - If one stands relaxed with bat in hand, one can rock one's shoulders up and down like a seesaw, and there is no tension.

Dimension 2 - Likewise, if one stands relaxed with bat in hand, one can twist one's front shoulder forward while bending one's back shoulder back, again without causing real tension.

Dimension 3 - But if both moves are combined (called the crank), suddenly there is persistent tension in the whole upper body, like rubber bands being stretched. The more you exaggerate the combined moves – by pulling the front shoulder down and forward with your underarm side muscles, and by keeping the rear shoulder elevated and bent backward using the back muscles - the tighter the rubber bands feel.

The crank's "static energy" is the building block for the swing.

Using one's core, "Static" crank tension intensifies during the "Step" stage, while striding towards the pitcher. Unwinding the crank during the "Go" stage grooves the bat to strike the ball in a "squared up" manner, releasing the energy.

Lets first look at the "static" crank elements.

Tris Speaker (center), in 1915, .345 life time BA

Alex Rodriguez

Shoulders –*A Rod* has a moderate crank pose, pulling down in front and pulling the rear shoulder back to wind the body up.

Elbows – While cranking up, his elbows are bent_and hands kept back to prevent hitching dips.

Legs – With his torso cranked, Alex's legs are pulled together, poised slightly on his back foot

Knees – The knees are flexed and tilted inside the ankles, causing additional tension and a low center of gravity.

Hands – The hands do not move.

The Step Stage

Once the Crank is in place, and the body holds a ball of energy, it is time to super-size it. *The step* multiplies the Crank's unit of energy, and the multiple depends on the size of the step one takes, and the discipline to control it all through one's core muscles.

Young hitters take small 3-inch steps or no step at all, as stepping without first cranking, throws them off balance, But if one starts with the crank and then steps, the rubber bands inside of you stretch further, and a huge reservoir of energy is built up, ready to explode upon the incoming ball.

Professionals step as far as needed based upon pitch count and other circumstances to exploit bodily physics. Most of the time, professionals first load off of the back leg so that they can drive the front leg out as far as possible. Most stride 24 inches or more, creating more than a 3 foot spread between the feet before the swing trigger is pulled.

Also, the load element is solely a back leg phenomenon, having nothing to do with lifting one's hands. During the whole load and step moment, the hands don't move, even though the step tension begs for their release. Instead, hand/body separation is achieved by moving the body forward, away from the hands, the core in command. Let's look at the elements of the step stage of the swing..

The Load – Still cranked up, Mike lifts his front leg to create as much pent up energy as possible on the back leg and hip.

Mike Trout
(big step)

His side muscles are pulling his front shoulder down to meet his kick leg, intensifying the "static" crank position.

He will step 24+ inches straight towards the pitcher, with his toes angled forward 45 degrees.

The Step – Dustin's 45-degree step turns his ankle and knee, opening up the front hip. Unturned ankle/knee joints lock you up, impeding the coming pivot move.

Dustin Pedroia
(Giant step!)

Once Dustin's lead hip is open like this, and the static energy of the crank has been multiplied by the massive stretch of his three-foot stride, there is only one path his body can take to release the energy. This "gate swinging" path is described next as the "go" stage of the swing.

The Go Stage

With all the "static" crank & step energy built up inside, it's time to use one's core, channel it to the ball, <u>and nowhere else</u>.

The "Go" stage unwinds the energy, directed to deliver the greatest impact possible without using the arms or hands as extra impulses. Arm/hand additions destabilize the swing by fractions of an inch, causing one to not hit the ball squarely. The core triggers the swing, and the arms/hands follow close behind the rotating body, a single stabilized configuration of bodily elements.

If you crank and step properly (meaning to the full extent possible using you core as the driver), then the "go" stage requires very little planning. Your body is positioned so that it can <u>only</u> pivot by turning on the front shoulder, letting the back hip swing around like a gate.

Once pivoted, both the body and the bat "square up"; they become perpendicular to the pitcher and the incoming ball. The hands are still cocked, as they were at the start of the turn, and the elbows are still bent as they were in the initial stance, one with the core. These details do not need to be micro-managed; they fall in line naturally, <u>if you cranked and stepped properly in the first place.</u>

In this "squared up" state, one "bats" the ball, using a push move, with the chest giving one last bit of push energy at contact.

Finally, when all of the energy has been "pushed out" to the incoming ball, one should lift the bat (don't swing it, lift it) up to your shoulder. This assures that your chest participated in the final delivery of energy. In real time this all appears to be a circular swing, but it is really a push and lift. Push and lift is "batting", whereas pirouetting is "spin-hitting" at best. Let's look at the elements within the "go" stage.

Harmon Killebrew

Pivot – *Pete* – all cranked up, initiates the turn by stepping and pivoting via his core around the front shoulder (not the head).

He swings the back hip out - like a gate - to eventually square up to the pitcher.

Pete Rose

Pete's whole hand/arm/torso configuration is unified through the turn; head back, quiet eyes, uniform elbow bends, the hands along for the ride, never trying to race his hands against the body while unwinding the crank.

In circling 'round, *Pete's* wrists always remain cocked, in a push positio. They have not been rolled over, as that would dissipate energy before striking the ball.

Weight Transfer – As *Mike* un-cranks, his weight transfer does not spin like a top; it moves perpendicular towards the incoming ball. The hip pivot points his back knee at the pitcher. This outcome is the result of a proper crank and step; his body wants to move forward.

Mike Trout

Stay Unified - *Jeter* keeps his head "frozen" behind the ball even as the weight transfer occurs. He keeps the swing plane at the angle of the incoming ball, keeping his hips even. He stays forward; doesn't stand up and never leans back.

Derek Jeter

Squaring Up – Once *Robinson's* weight is carried on his front leg, and his body becomes perpendicular to the pitcher, the bat also naturally squares up to the incoming target, with the elbows <u>remaining slightly bent</u>, ready to meet the ball. He has not let the hand, elbow and torso configuration unwind, even minutely.

Robinson Cano

Payload Delivery – *Robinson* strikes the ball while his elbows are still bent, thrusting his chest <u>forward</u>. The body's full payload is delivered at the moment of bat/ball impact, just like striking the heavy bag.

Robinson Cano

Back End Release - When ready to meet the ball, *Bryce* simultaneously releases any remaining back end energy. He stays balanced using his back toe, which for a moment floats in the air.

Bryce Harper

Follow Through – With both hands on the bat; Bryce <u>lifts </u>the bat up to his shoulder, thus keeping the chest fully engaged in the body's forward, perpendicular momentum sequence.

Bryce Harper

The Last Drop - *Dustin* holds on tight, not letting the bat spin away, exploiting any final chest-thrusting energy his body can muster.

Dustin Pedroia

Rest The Bat – Most of the time, if your swing is balanced and efficient, all of the energy was delivered forward and the bat can now lie comfortably on your shoulder. Here, there is no tension left in *Robinson's* body wanting to snap the bat back.

Robinson Cano

"Ditto" Ted Williams   *"Ditto" Reggie Jackson*

Chicago 1935

Umpire Jeff Nelson

BP

PART 3
PAST MASTERS

Ted Williams, a bit more upright than with most of his swings,
hence a twisted back foot – but the photo is amazing.

Upon landing, *Ted's toe is at 45 degrees, his* weight is straddled across both legs, but energy is collected, ready to burst. He pivots on the front shoulder and the hand, arm, torso configuration begins to swing towards the pitcher. The weight stays forward until the end

Ted Williams (normal finish, back leg, knee pointed towards pitcher)

Babe Ruth (BTW, The Babe" moved his hands slightly
when loading up on his back leg for timing – below: foot leaving ground)

Jackie Robinson (above: His follow through balance, chest out – below: front foot opens hips, and his bat rests on his shoulder at finish)

"Jolten" Joe Dimaggio (his 56 game batting streak)

Holy Cow!

Hank Aaron (100% perfect) – A Yogism – takes a huge step!

The home run king!

Willie Mays (huge step, front pivot, chest out)

Say Hey!

Mickey Mantle

5 foot, 10 inches tall hitting a 500 footer while batting over 300.

Roger Maris   *Mickey Mantle*

George Brett (elbows stay bent through rotation)

Cal Ripken Jr. (elbows bent, weight stays forward)
The ironman – he showed up.

Rickey Henderson (my role model) – 100 lead off home runs. Greatest leadoff hitter and base runner of all time. Said low leg load helped him see incoming ball.

Wade Boggs – Crank, Step and Go. Never abandoned his hands/elbows/torso unity while rotating – never!

Weight moving forward, not back, not up, not to the side.

Rod Carew - smooth as silk, never loses his cool,
won't over swing, pivots on his front shoulder, hands kept close.

His special stance

Tony Gwynn (classic – weight moves forward, back leg floats)

Roger Hornsby (number 2 batting average of all time).
Totally forward – toe floats.

Totally forward!

Reggie Jackson – Mr October with a more-than-complete follow through, really getting his chest into it.

Swinging for the fences: three home runs in game 6 to win the 1977 World Series (Lived in my NYC neighborhood; same coffee shop; we would nod at each other).

He Pivots & unwinds   *Cranked & loaded*

Chest out   *It's gone!*

Crank it up!   *Multiply the crank!*

Release the crank   *Release it all*

Lou Gherig
Say no more

David Ortiz – Big Papi
Crank It Up!

Yankee Stadium – *That's Maris striking the ball, pushing out, elbows still bent, back foot dragging, with Mantle on deck.*

I was there!

Play Ball!

PART 4
SITUATIONAL HITTING

As described in the previous sections, batting mechanics boil down to just three components: Crank, Step and Go. In contrast, once in the batter's box, pitch-by-pitch, a host of chess-like variables descend, making it tough to get hits!

Nowadays, MLB players rarely have batting averages over .300, Even if one's crank, step and go mechanics are clean and one's mind steels itself for the situational chess match, players still fail 7-8 out of 10 times. 96-mile an hour fastballs have a way of humiliating the best no matter how well they mentally prepare for each pitch. But if not mentally prepared, a batter's effectiveness falls further.

This chapter attempts to make order of the many variables batters face, towards devising a situational batting framework. It is quite a maze. For example, what is the wisdom of when to take the first pitch? Ok, there will be a lot of opinions here from various readers, but here goes!

A rookie facing Bob Gibson

Batter's Temperament & Field Configuration

The first variable to consider is the batter's core abilities – Is "he" a good contact hitter, a power hitter; is he prone to striking out, or both. Can he bunt, and is he fast? Is he reliable?

A batter's potential then breaks down further - better in day games or night games - better at home or on the road? How effective are they at different pitch counts? Can they hit to the opposite field?

Next, the number of combinations of offense and defense players on the field has many possibilities. There can be any combination of zero, one or two out situations against the various base runner combinations, such as: no base runners, runner on first, runner on second, runners on first and second, etc. There are 24 out/runner combinations.

Added to this is the placement of the defense. Is the infield playing in or out? Is the outfield deep or shallow? Is there a shift on?

Having A Plan

Different ability/field and pitch count combinations affect the batter's goal for the very next pitch. Are you hitting away or are you in a "small ball" situation, trying to move runners into scoring position and drive them in?

Let's first look at hitting away topics and then examine "small ball" factors thereafter.

Hitting Away

With nobody on base, one is usually hitting away, though guys like Ricky Henderson also bunt for singles. In a hitting away circumstance, most batters prefer straight fastballs, a one-dimensional challenge of catching up to the ball. Other pitches – sinkers, curves, sliders and knuckleballs – require exquisite timing and calibrated swing plane adjustments to hit the round ball with the round bat as the ball moves non-linearly.

Non-linear ball movement is trouble!

So one looks for (hopes for) a "straight-shooting" fastball whenever it is the next probable pitch – meaning when a pitcher cannot afford to miss with "moving pitches" that can go astray. The fastball pitch counts are: 0-0, 1-0, 2-0, 2-1, 3-0, 3-1. In these situations, batters get to zone in, and wait for "their" pitch. If the incoming is a good strike, then one should gratefully turn on it, as one probably only gets one good pitch per at bat.

This one good pitch reality leads to the opening question: Should one swing at the first pitch? The answer is definitely YES, if that's your one good pitch per at bat coming at you.

By the way, check out *www.fangraphs.com* for MLB data patterns over the past decade, showing that today batters pass on more and more first pitches, and in turn get themselves into count deficits, achieving diminished output as a result. In today's MLB, the 0-1 and 0-2 counts are at a 25-year high.

In 1988 15% of first pitches were put in play whereas only 11% were put into play by 2012. This 4% decrease of in play first pitches resulted in a 7% increase in strikes, with balls decreasing the other 3%. Which implies: If they won't swing, throw more strikes.

In the teen games I am involved with, when the opposing pitcher lands a first pitch right down the middle, the comforting response from the dugout is "now you've seen it." My response to this is "and you won't see it again."

The general problem with fastballs, though, is that they're fast, making them difficult to time. But during the GO stage, by keeping the bat plane at the same angle as the incoming ball, this timing obstacle is mitigated. If the ball and bat are traversing within the same plane, then one can make contact with the ball at many junctures within that plane. If you are ahead of the pitch the ball is pulled at contact, if late the ball travels to the opposite field.

But to achieve this, the batter's torso/arms/hand configuration needs to stay in place during the entire gate swinging rotation. You get one move to the ball and you need to keep the turn extremely stable to make solid contact. And certainly you don't get two moves – as in a "hitch" – when one first moves the hands up, down or backwards to wind up for the swing. If one hitches, one needs to time both the hitch and the swing to somehow find the ball, and find it within the ball's travel plane as it moves anywhere from 70 to 100 mph.

Kids get away with hitch windups, as the fastballs they face are not that fast, so they actually have the time to mess around with wind up moves while the ball is travelling. But on the big field, as pitching climbs into the 80 and 90 mph ranges, there simply is not enough time for multiple moves to the ball.

Referring back to the previous chapters, the body's collective STEP dynamics trigger the GO Step's energy release, not some tiny move of the hands. The STEP separates the hands from the body by moving the body forward, leaving the still hands behind.

Some young hitters, wanting to separate the hands from the body, confuse keeping the hands still - with the inverse - keeping the body still while MOVING THE HANDS BACKWARD, a complicated backward windup "hitch" - which cannot be timed with real pitching.

Alternatively, if one attains a stable GO step - a smooth turning of the gate without complicating digressions – one can begin to channel the intensity or tempo of the swing. Until then one merely hacks at the ball.

Tempo is essential with dangerous 0-2, 1-2 counts, where one *intends* contact, either fouling off or putting the ball into play. There is no need for home run swings in these moments unless you were born and bred to do this (e.g. REGGIE JACKSON).

Even when hitting away, one needs to read the lay of the land, and pick the correct objective: a base hit or something more, and tempo determines the swing intensity (e.g. choking up).

There is an expression "Look for the fastball and wait on the curve." Curve balls give you a pinch of time to adjust if you are patient. Conversely if one looks for a curve and gets a fastball, the fastball will shoot by without having time to adjust to it.

And besides regular curve balls, there are off speed curves, sliders and screwballs to contend with, plus straight change ups and the occasional knuckleball. So you need to know the pitcher's arsenal and habits. What is his preferred strike out pitch? Try and foul it off. (Catfish Hunter, master tactician).

No matter the pitch type, one doesn't want to chase balls out of the strike zone. Any pitch making the batter stand up or causing one to unravel the torso, arm, elbow, hand configuration is usually out of the strike zone. If you feel you are unraveling, don't swing or check your swing.

Many of the action photos of the previous chapter illustrate just how well the great hitters maintain their form throughout the swing. By deeply feeling their form, they can sense when an incoming pitch is drawing them to unravel, and they reject this bad feeling and do not swing. Rejecting a pitch becomes more of a total-body feeling than an intellectual exercise.

Similarly, by relying on feeling, great hitters pass on strikes they cannot drive. They would rather face an 0-2 count then dribble a difficult 0-1 pitch to the shortstop.

The last thing I'll say about swinging away is to consider the depth of the outfield. If the outfield is playing deep, then really bear down to look for a line drive or a hard hit bouncer up the middle. If they are shallow, give it a ride. Most young players have one swing, and they hope for the best.

Small Ball

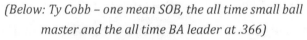

(Below: Ty Cobb – one mean SOB, the all time small ball master and the all time BA leader at .366)

One or two runs usually win good baseball games. "Small Ball" is the art of using "productive outs" to move runners into scoring position and drive them in – collecting one run at a time. Productive outs are outs that score a run or at least advance base runners. Striking out is not productive, hitting a deep fly allowing the runner to tag up at third is very productive.

Nowadays in the MLB, small ball has been fading. The main reason is that most of the players can hit with power, and statistics prove that giving up "productive" outs is less effective than swinging away. With power hitters, scoring with a man on first and <u>no</u> outs is more likely than scoring with a man on second and <u>one</u> out. But this is the MLB where everyone is a machine. Small ball still works with teen baseball.

Hit and Run

Hitting behind the runner (hitting the ball between first and second) is standard fare in small ball, but it is most effective in what's called the "hit and run", where the runner takes off trusting that the batter will make good contact with the incoming pitch. Earlier in this section the question of the batters' reliability was mentioned. Can the batter be counted on to smack the ball into the ground assuming the pitch is anywhere near the strike zone? Few coaches spend time drilling hitters to achieve hit and run sacrifices, and hence, very little small ball is pursued even at the varsity level.

Also, small ball calls for aggressive play, which some avoid.

Below: Rose hits Fosse in the 1970 all star game.

Bunting

Bunting for hits, sacrifice bunts and squeeze bunts are three small ball weapons that put pressure on defenses. To counter a good bunt by a fast runner, the defensive player usually needs to take a bit of risk in charging and fielding the ball, and further risk in throwing the ball before the fielder's feet are comfortably set. Bunting requires defensive perfection to shut bunting down.

I am always amazed that in teen ball, bunting is left behind, and that like hit and run drills, bunting drills are not conducted. If a player has speed, a first inning bunt-for-hit attempt tests out the opponent team's ability to deal with the challenge. Until opponents show they can shut down the bunt, every fast guy on the bench should be told to bunt.

Surely sacrifice bunting – moving runners to second and third – is a no brainer with less than two outs, but again, the batter needs to be able to deliver the bunt "in his sleep"! Bunting requires reliance, and reliance comes with bunting drills.

The squeeze bunt – getting the guy on third home – is not so easy in the major leagues, but in teen ball, it usually requires the basic ability to bunt and the runner's awareness on when to take off. Most defenses cannot cope with this pressure, especially as the incoming runner represents a brute physical force coming at the catcher. Again, squeeze bunting comes down to drilling the team, generally making all bunt events common place.

The fundamentals of bunting include the following: One sets up at the top of the batter's box, getting one closer to first base, and making it problematic for the pitcher to get a low curve to sink out of range. One can "show" the bunt right away to get the infield to react, giving the runner a slight lead advantage, or one can square to bunt late, once the pitcher's front foot lands. One needs to pivot and square up, else one ends up waving at the pitch with one's eyes seeing the ball at a bit of an angle, rather than straight on. Let the ball strike the bat, rather than pushing the bat, so that your strike point does not move. Run like hell to maximize the pressure on the defense.

Of course one can simply steal home – Jackie Robinson & Yogi

Sacrifice Flies

Getting runners in from third via a sacrifice fly need not be all luck. Good hitters can produce fly balls by moderating their swing tempo, with a smaller step and a simple pivot during the go moment. This too can be practiced.

And so, that is a bit on small ball. Now let's wrap it up with one more comment.

Knowing The Pitcher

Finally, one should come to the plate with a bit of awareness regarding the pitcher. What is the pitcher's "out" pitch? What did you learn from the last at bat? What pitch is working today? What is the breaking ball's movement, and sensing change ups that appear to be fastballs?

Try hitting this! - Dizzy Dean

The Wrap Up - No hits, no runs, no errors, no nothin'

All in all, there are so many intellectual issues to incorporate during the game that a batter has little chance of succeeding if their Crank, Step and Go forms are not locked in. Coming to the plate with chaotic warm up swings to get loose is the worst, as rather than feeling the form, one instead paints an undisciplined pattern in both one's mind and body.

So stay grounded. Stay focused. Stay aware.

Good luck!

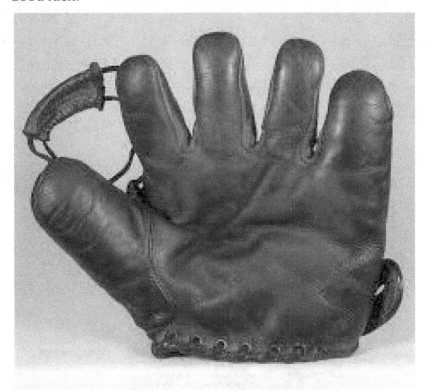

PART 5
BATTING DRILLS

Ok, so the Crank, Step and Go batting sequence described earlier represents the foundation forms one should embody. But how to make these forms second nature, baked into one's muscle memory is another matter.

After consulting with a few college coaches, and watching videos of Robinson Cano working out in the off season, a ten-minute, seven-cycle drill evolved using inexpensive equipment that does not require a batting practice pitcher. If followed rigorously, this daily conditioning drill can re-tool a little league "spin" hitter into a proper adult "rotational" hitter.

Below: The ten-minute, Seven Step Cycle – repeat numerous times a day. You need a heavy boxing bag and a swing away unit, together costing around $400. Complementing the seven drills, one should add soft toss and cage pitching as steps eight and nine if cage and pitching resources are available.

And, of course, daily one needs to work on flexibility and conditioning.

Giancarlo Stanton working his core.

First Exercise: 10 "Heavy Bag" Swings –
To awaken and engage your core as the glue to your swing mechanics.

Standing at the heavy bag all cranked up, but not frozen, use your stomach muscles (your core) to unwind the crank, causing the hands to drop to the imaginary target rather than fan out. Keep the core engaged through the bottom of the swing as the bat begins to climb to the angle of the imagined incoming ball. Notice that when swinging with an engaged core, one's wrists do not feel weak when striking the bag. Robinson Cano holds a 50-pound weight to his chest and rotates his core with the added weight to build "core dominance", others swing bats in water.

Above: Robinson Cano "exercises" his core in a game situation.

Second Exercise: 10 "Feet in Cement" Swings –
To hone an elliptical bat path that stays connected to one's core.

At the swing away unit, plant your feet apart as though you just took your step, and keep them grounded flat, as if standing in cement. Focus on the elliptical path of the bat from release of the crank, to striking the ball, to the follow through onto the landing shoulder. Without the use of one's legs, one is forced to swing the bat on the correct elliptical path without sweeping away from the body before contact or pulling towards the body after contact.

Hank Aaron

When swinging freely (not in cement), non-elliptical imbalances are masked by offset movements in the feet or in the follow through of the arms and upper body. Keeping the feet "cemented" groves the swing to avoid imbalances in the first place.

Do not over swing. Stay relaxed. Let the body supply the power within the perfect ellipse.

Third Exercise: 10 "Light the Match" Swings –
To release the back end of your body in a stable manner.

(Above: Bret, Right: Bench)

At the swing away unit, with your feet apart as above, swing as above, but release your back foot so that it scrapes the ground like a match on a striking area. The foot should not twist but should glide straight to the pitcher, your back knee also pointing to the pitcher. An incorrect bat path will pull you off balance, forcing the foot/knee "rudder" off target as compensation.

Feet imbalances mainly occur due to an incomplete follow through of the upper body, causing the feet to inversely shift to maintain overall stability. If one follows through all the way to one's shoulder, even to the extent that one "rests the bat" on the shoulder, then all energy has been released, thereby requiring no twisted offsets by the feet.

One cannot "rest the bat" if one over swings, causing tightness in the ellipse. Stay relaxed, let the core drive the ball.

Fourth Exercise: 10 "Full" Swings – To feel the combined effects of the above exercises.

Now that one's core, one's bat path and a relaxed follow-through have been etched into the swing, maintain these forms as you swing away. Feel power at ball impact from the accelerated drop of the hands amplified by the stability and thrust of the core.

Release all of the energy by releasing the upper body to fully rotate the bat until it rests quietly on one's shoulder. Don't snap the bat back; rest it. If snapping back, everything is too tight and energy meant for the ball, stays trapped inside the body.

(Photos Robinson and Harper)

A second facet of swinging away is to grove the step. Many just step forward landing the foot at a 45-degree angle. Bryce Harper, during the step "shows" the bottom of the front foot to the pitcher, causing a deeper load dynamic on his back leg. Unwinding this full ankle turn yields him better cadence and energy. Try it while at your swing away unit.

Fifth Exercise: 10 "Front Arm Only" Swings –
To ensure the front arm is not pulling or pushing the overall swing.

When squaring up to strike the ball, one essentially pushes perpendicularly through the ball, rather than swinging in a wide arc around the ball. In this push moment, one's back hand is the leader of the actual push dynamic, with the front hand participating as a "helper", pulling – not pushing.

The "front arm only" exercise makes sure that the front arm is doing its part. If the front arm is lazy, it will slow or steer the push move off course, while also short changing energy delivered to the ball at impact.

Many young hitters trying "front hand" using a swing away unit cannot even hit the ball and instead hit the elastic bands holding the ball. One should religiously work this exercise towards the goal of never missing the center of the ball, ever!

Crank up with the front hand holding the bat and the back hand bracing (not gripping) the bat around mid-bat. Next un-crank using one's core, while controlling the bat pat with the front hand, snapping the wrist exactly at ball impact, not before or after.

Sixth Exercise: 10 "Drop the Bat" Swings –
To reinforce keeping the arms and hands close to the core to maximize overall body/extremity cohesion.

Many players have difficulty eliminating the old habit of pirouetting around with both hands circling out to the ball. "Drop the Bat" causes one to instead keep the hands close to the core, and to attack the ball in a down and then up elliptical bat path.

Crank up as usual, but before initiating the swing with your core, loosen your grip so that the bat slides down around six inches before gripping it again. Once in this exaggerated choking-up position, initiate the swing. The motion upon striking the ball has the appearance of a baton twirling upwards.

The spot that you caught the bat is actually the optimal swing launching position assuring the bat does not get caught getting off the shoulder, and the baton motion requires one to keep the bat path uniformly attached to the core from launch to land.

Hit the ball right as the baton motion starts lifting up.

Seventh Exercise: 10 : "Walk Up" Swings –
To capture all forward energy upon striking the ball.

This exercise reinforces one thing: direct all momentum back to the pitcher. Simply set up three steps back and walk up to the swing away unit, striking the ball once in proximity, and then taking one more step forward just to make the forward momentum point stick.

Eighth Exercise: 20 "Soft Toss" Swings –
keep the form as you incorporate a moving ball.

Ninth Exercise: 20 "BP Cage" Swings –
take 20 throws in the cage from a BP partner. Keep the form.

Ok, That's about 100+ swings all together, now get back on line and do it again.

Below: La Dodger training camp

Below: guess who these guys are.

MLB STATISTICS

Batting average	*.342*
Hits	*2,873*
Home runs	*714*
Runs batted in	*2,213*
Win–loss record	*94–46*
Earned run average	*2.28*

Baseball in America Lyrics

As promised, here are the Baseball in America lyrics written for the Miracle League.

We play baseball ... in America

Learn to keep our eye on the ball

Yea we play baseball here in America

And now there's a field accessible to all

So let me see your overhand ball

Let me see you swing for the wall

Let me see you there, going for it all

And so we're here together

Standing tall

American made, just like our baseball

And when inside the batter's box

At the Miracle League

It's your turn to be what you can be

Come on, Come on

Come on, Come on

Above – Baseball from Shiloh Battlefield - 1862

We Play Baseball in America
Abner Doubleday and the boys, 1863

CPSIA information can be obtained
at www.ICGtesting.com
Printed in the USA
BVHW070715030919
557429BV00001B/81/P